Abraham Lincoln

Civil War President

By John Perritano

Children's Press®
An Imprint of Scholastic Inc.

Content Consultant
Samuel Wheeler, Ph.D., State Historian of Illinois
Director of Research and Collections, Abraham Lincoln Presidential Library & Museum

Thank you to Jevon Bolden for her insights into African American history and culture.

Library of Congress Catalog-in-Publication Data
Names: Perritano, John, author.
Title: Abraham Lincoln: Civil War President/by John Perritano.
Description: New York: Children's Press, an imprint of Scholastic Inc., 2021. | Series: Presidential biographies | Includes index. | Audience: Ages 7-9. | Audience: Grades 2-3. | Summary: "Book introduces the reader to Abraham Lincoln and his life."— Provided by publisher.
Identifiers: LCCN 2020002636 | ISBN 9780531130988 (library binding) | ISBN 9780531130704 (paperback)
Subjects: LCSH: Lincoln, Abraham, 1809-1865—Juvenile literature. | Presidents—United States—Biography—Juvenile literature. | United States—History—Civil War, 1861-1865—Juvenile literature. | United States—Politics and government—1861-1865—Juvenile literature.
Classification: LCC E457.45 .P47 2021 | DDC 973.7092 [B]—dc23
LC record available at https://lccn.loc.gov/2020002636

Initial prototype design by Anna Tunick Tabachnik
Produced by Spooky Cheetah Press
Design by Kimberly Shake

No part of this publication may be reproduced in whole or in part, or stored in a retrieval system, or transmitted in any form or by any means, electronic, mechanical, photocopying, recording, or otherwise, without written permission of the publisher. For information regarding permission, write to Scholastic Inc., Attention: Permissions Department, Scholastic Inc., 557 Broadway, New York, NY 10012.
© 2021 Scholastic Inc.

All rights reserved. Published in 2021 by Children's Press, an imprint of Scholastic Inc.

Printed in North Mankato, MN, USA 113

SCHOLASTIC, CHILDREN'S PRESS, PRESIDENTIAL BIOGRAPHIES™, and associated logos are trademarks and/or registered trademarks of Scholastic Inc.

1 2 3 4 5 6 7 8 9 10 R 30 29 28 27 26 25 24 23 22 21

Scholastic Inc., 557 Broadway, New York, NY 10012.

Photos ©: cover, spine portrait: Sarin Images/The Granger Collection; back cover lincoln: The Granger Collection; 4 icon and throughout: Anthony Berger/Library of Congress; 5: Mathew B. Brady/Library of Congress; 6: The Granger Collection; 7: Ingram Publishing/Getty Images; 8: Bettmann/Getty Images; 10: Sarin Images/The Granger Collection; 11: Bettmann/Getty Images; 13: Jim McMahon/Mapman ®; 14: The Granger Collection; 15: Library of Congress; 16: Bob Thomas/Popperfoto/Getty Images; 17 bill: Les Cunliffe/Dreamstime; 17 coin: eldadcarin/Getty Images; 19: Buyenlarge/UIG/age fotostock; 20: Bettmann/Getty Images; 21: Matthew Brady/Buyenlarge/Getty Images; 22: Mark Maritato/Bridgeman Images; 23: Bridgeman Images; 26: George Eastman Museum/Getty Images; 28: Jasmina/Dreamstime; 29: Scene in the House on the Passage of the Proposition to Amend the Constitution, January 31, 1865., Harper's Weekly, 1865-02-18, Collection of the U.S. House of Representatives; 30 top left: Universal History Archive/UIG/Shutterstock; 30 top right: GraphicaArtis/Getty Images; 30 bottom center: Ingram Publishing/Getty Images; 30 bottom right: Bettmann/Getty Images; 31 top left: The Art Archive/Shutterstock; 31 top center: Bridgeman Images; 31 bottom left: Library of Congress; 31 bottom right: George Eastman Museum/Getty Images.

All other photos © Shutterstock.

COVER: A photo of Lincoln from November 1863.

SOURCE NOTES: Page 13: Abraham Lincoln's letter to Henry L. Pierce and others, April 6, 1859, in *The Collected Works of Abraham Lincoln*, ed. by Roy P. Basler et al., accessed at http://www.abrahamlincolnonline.org/lincoln/speeches/pierce.htm; page 14: "House Divided Speech," Illinois Republican State Convention, Springfield, Illinois, June 16, 1858, in Mark E. Neely Jr., *The Abraham Lincoln Encyclopedia* (New York: Da Capo Press, 1982), accessed at https://www.nps.gov/liho/learn/historyculture/housedivided.htm; page 22: Gettysburg Address, November 19, 1863, National Consitution Center, accessed at https://constitutioncenter.org/blog/read-six-different-versions-of-the-gettysburg-address; page 25: Abraham Lincoln, Abraham Lincoln papers: Series 3, General Correspondence, 1837 to 1897: Abraham Lincoln, [March 4, 1865], (Second Inaugural Address, endorsed by Lincoln April 10, 1865), accessed at https://www.loc.gov/item/mal4361300

Table of Contents

CHAPTER 1
Meet Abe Lincoln 4
Humble Beginnings 7
Young Mr. Lincoln 9
On to Congress 11

CHAPTER 2
A House Divided 12
Slavery Tears at the Nation 15
Mr. President 17

CHAPTER 3
The Country at War 18
Fighting for Freedom 21
Turning Point at Gettysburg 23

CHAPTER 4
Healing the Nation's Wounds 24
Lincoln's Last Days 27

▶ **In Depth:** *The 13th Amendment Ends Slavery* 28
▶ **Timeline** 30
▶ **Glossary** 32
▶ **Index** 32

CHAPTER 1

Meet Abe Lincoln

Abraham Lincoln was our 16th president. At the time of his presidency, the country was sharply divided. **Slavery** was legal in the South, but not in the North. As the country grew, so did arguments about whether slavery should expand into new territories.

Soon this fight over slavery sparked the U.S. Civil War. The North (Union) battled the South (Confederates) for four bloody years. The conflict almost tore our country in half for good.

Lincoln will always be remembered for holding the nation together and for freeing millions of enslaved African Americans. In fact, many people say Abraham Lincoln was one of the greatest presidents in U.S. history.

Lincoln was 52 years old when he took office.

The Civil War raged from 1861 to 1865. It lasted Lincoln's entire presidency.

As a young man, Lincoln often kept a book with him so he could read during breaks from work.

Humble Beginnings

Abraham Lincoln was born on February 12, 1809, in Kentucky. His family lived in a tiny log cabin that had a dirt floor.

Lincoln's dad was a farmer. Abe helped plow fields and plant seeds. He split wood rails for fences. Because Lincoln was always helping at home, he could not attend school regularly. All together, he had only about one year of formal education. Still, Lincoln tried to learn as much as he could on his own.

Lincoln's mother died when he was nine, and his father soon remarried. Abe's stepmother, Sarah, encouraged his love of reading.

This is what Lincoln's childhood home looked like.

Because of his early work cutting wood for fences, Lincoln was later known as "the Rail Splitter."

Lincoln was big and strong. He often ran in races and was a wrestling champ.

Young Mr. Lincoln

Lincoln worked at all sorts of jobs. When he wasn't working at home, his father hired him out to work for neighbors. Abe didn't keep the money he earned, though. That was used to help support the family.

Lincoln's family moved a lot in search of good farmland. They settled in Illinois when Abe was 21. That is when Lincoln finally left home. He had many jobs, including postmaster, and even managed a store.

Abe met a teacher who asked him to join a **debate** club. It was a good way to learn how to speak about important issues. Lincoln eventually gained fame as a great speaker.

Lincoln dedicated a lot of time to educating himself. He even taught himself enough to become a lawyer by the time he was 27.

As a lawyer, Lincoln argued cases in courts across Illinois.

Lincoln rode from courthouse to courthouse on horseback. One of his horses was named Old Tom.

On to Congress

Lincoln was also interested in politics. In 1834, he ran for the Illinois state **legislature**, called the General Assembly, and won. Lincoln helped make laws for his state. He was reelected three times.

During this time, Abe met Mary Todd. Both loved poetry and politics. The couple married in 1842 and eventually had four sons together. They lived in Springfield, Illinois.

In 1846, Lincoln was elected to the U.S. House of Representatives. He was representing his state in the U.S. Congress. That is the branch of government that makes laws for our country.

Mary Todd was from Lincoln's home state of Kentucky.

CHAPTER 2

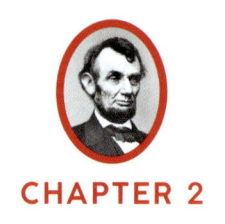

A House Divided

Lincoln's two-year **term** as a congressman ended. Then he returned to practicing law. But the issue of slavery pulled him back into politics before long.

In the South, enslaved people were forced to work in homes and businesses and on large farms. They had no rights or freedoms. In the North, slavery was against the law. Many people wanted it **abolished**.

America was growing. Territories were added in the western part of the country. Many people feared slavery would spread into these new lands. Back in 1820, Congress had passed a law called the Missouri Compromise. The government decided which new states would allow slavery and which would be free.

The Missouri Compromise, 1820

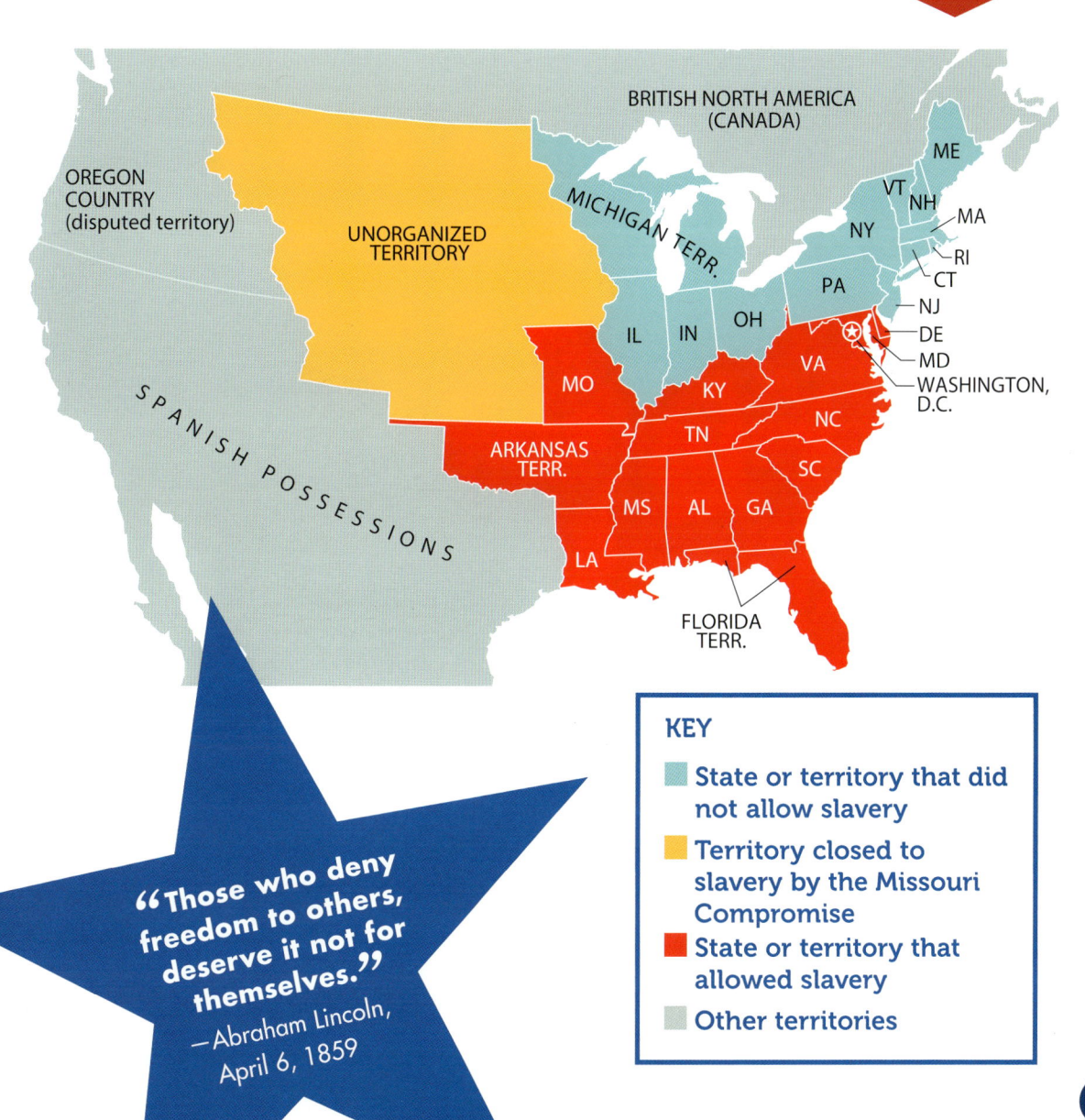

The Missouri Compromise controlled where slavery would be allowed in the United States.

Map labels:
- OREGON COUNTRY (disputed territory)
- UNORGANIZED TERRITORY
- BRITISH NORTH AMERICA (CANADA)
- MICHIGAN TERR.
- SPANISH POSSESSIONS
- ME, VT, NH, MA, NY, RI, CT, PA, NJ, DE, MD, WASHINGTON, D.C.
- IL, IN, OH, VA, MO, KY, NC, ARKANSAS TERR., TN, SC, MS, AL, GA, LA, FLORIDA TERR.

KEY
- State or territory that did not allow slavery
- Territory closed to slavery by the Missouri Compromise
- State or territory that allowed slavery
- Other territories

> "Those who deny freedom to others, deserve it not for themselves."
> —Abraham Lincoln, April 6, 1859

Lincoln faced Douglas in seven debates during 1858. A lot of people liked what Lincoln had to say.

"A house divided against itself cannot stand."
—Abraham Lincoln, June 16, 1858

14

Slavery Tears at the Nation

Thirty-four years after the Missouri Compromise, in 1854, Congress passed the Kansas–Nebraska Act. With the Missouri Compromise, the government had decided which territories would allow slavery. But the Kansas–Nebraska Act left it up to the people living in those territories to decide whether to allow slavery.

The law was Stephen Douglas's idea. He was a U.S. senator from Illinois. Lincoln didn't like the law. In 1858, he ran against Douglas in the race for the Senate. The two faced each other in a series of debates. Lincoln didn't win the election, but he made a big impression in the debates.

The debates between Lincoln and Douglas were so popular that they were later reenacted.

Lincoln was sworn into office on March 4, 1861.

At 6 feet, 4 inches tall, Lincoln is still the tallest U.S. president.

Mr. President

In early 1860, Lincoln decided to run for president. He won! People in the South were upset. They worried that Lincoln would abolish slavery. They said they would go to war to protect their right to enslave Black people.

In the month after the election, South Carolina **seceded** from the United States—also known as the Union. Lincoln was sworn into office the following March. By that time, six more southern states had joined South Carolina. They formed a government called the Confederate States of America.

On April 12, 1861, the Confederate army fired on a U.S. fort called Fort Sumter. The Civil War had begun.

Today, Lincoln's picture is on the penny and the five-dollar bill.

CHAPTER 3

The Country at War

The first thing Lincoln did was to call for 75,000 volunteers to serve in the Union army.

Many people believed the North would quickly win the war. The North had more soldiers. It had more guns. It had more money.

Those hopes were dashed on July 21, 1861. That day Union troops faced the Confederates for the first time at a small creek named Bull Run outside Washington, D.C.

The rebels were victorious. Defeated Union troops ran back to Washington. Everyone was shocked. People realized the war would be long.

During the Battle of Bull Run some people packed a picnic lunch to watch the fight. They had no idea how fierce the fighting would be.

The Union named battles for nearby waterways. That's why they called this the Battle of Bull Run. The South often named battles for nearby towns. They called this the Battle of Manassas.

Lincoln read the Emancipation Proclamation to his advisers before sharing it with the nation.

Lincoln's young sons Tad and Willie often burst into their father's office during important meetings.

20

Fighting for Freedom

The war turned bloodier as each month passed. Lincoln tried to find a general who would defeat the Confederate army. No one was up to the job. He thought the war would never end.

At first Lincoln fought the war solely to save the Union. But before long his war aims changed. Lincoln declared that Union troops would fight to end slavery.

On January 1, 1863, Lincoln issued the **Emancipation** Proclamation. This order said if the South did not rejoin the Union by January 1863, all enslaved people in all territories in rebellion would be freed.

Thomas, called Tad, was Abraham Lincoln's youngest son.

Usually, Union soldiers were identified by their blue jackets, and Confederates by their gray jackets. More than 50,000 were killed or wounded at the Battle of Gettysburg.

"... government of the people by the people for the people, shall not perish from the earth."
—Gettysburg Address, November 19, 1863

Turning Point at Gettysburg

In 1863, Confederate troops led by General Robert E. Lee invaded the North. The two armies met on July 1 at Gettysburg, Pennsylvania. For three days, the battle went back and forth. But ultimately the Union army was victorious. The war had finally turned in favor of the North. But it came at a high price. The Battle of Gettysburg was the bloodiest clash of the war.

That November, Lincoln dedicated a cemetery on the battlefield. He gave a short speech, which became known as the Gettysburg Address. In his speech, Lincoln restated America's founding ideals of democracy and freedom.

African Americans were able to join the Union army starting in 1863.

CHAPTER 4

Healing the Nation's Wounds

In 1864, Lincoln won a second term as president. He had hired and fired many generals during the war. No one, it seemed, could destroy the Confederate army. Finally, Lincoln put Ulysses S. Grant in charge. Grant followed Lee and his army, beating them in nearly every battle.

On March 4, 1865, when Lincoln took the oath of office for a second time, the war was almost over. He wanted to welcome the southern states back into the Union without punishing them harshly. He hoped to rebuild what had been destroyed. Others disagreed. They wanted to punish the South for its actions.

More than 30,000 people attended Lincoln's second inauguration in Washington, D.C.

President Lincoln

"... let us strive ... to bind up the nation's wounds ..."
—Abraham Lincoln, March 4, 1865

25

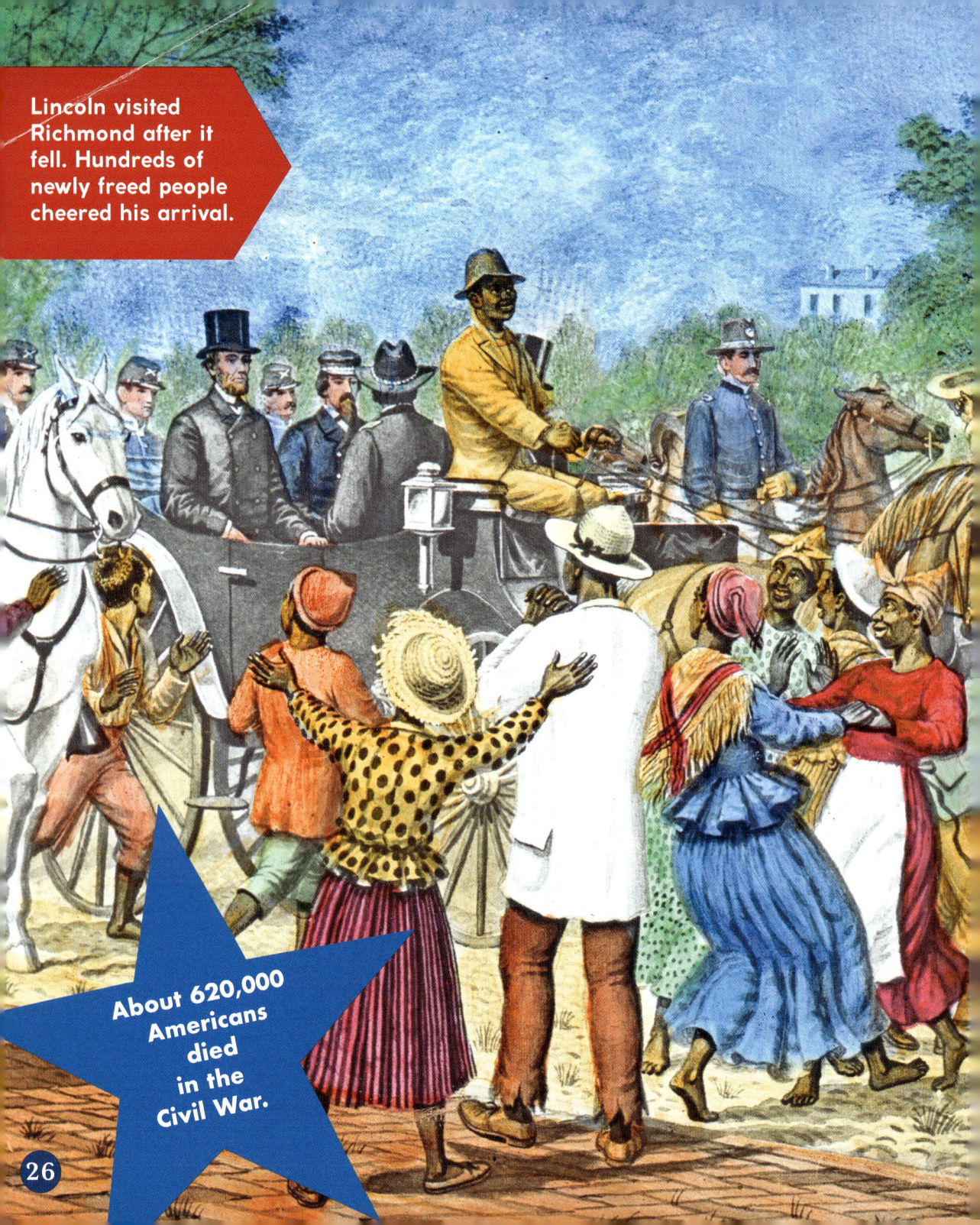

Lincoln visited Richmond after it fell. Hundreds of newly freed people cheered his arrival.

About 620,000 Americans died in the Civil War.

26

Lincoln's Last Days

On April 3, Richmond, Virginia, the capital of the Confederacy, fell to Union forces. On April 9, General Lee surrendered in Appomattox, Virginia.

On April 14, Lincoln celebrated the Union's victory by going to see a play at Ford's Theatre in Washington, D.C. An actor named John Wilkes Booth was waiting there. He blamed Lincoln for the South's losses. As Lincoln watched the play, Booth snuck up and shot him. The president died the next day.

In May, the last of the Confederate army surrendered. The war had taken a huge toll on the country. But Lincoln had saved the Union. He had freed more than four million people from the horrors of slavery. We remember and celebrate him to this day.

IN DEPTH

The 13th Amendment Ends Slavery

When Abraham Lincoln was first elected, he didn't believe the president had the authority to completely outlaw slavery. But by the end of the Civil War, Lincoln was determined to get rid of slavery once and for all.

To outlaw slavery, the Congress needed to change, or amend, the Constitution. Using all his skills as a speaker and politician, Lincoln pushed

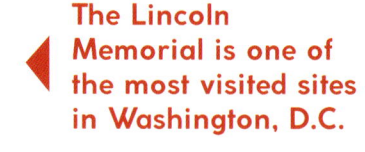

The Lincoln Memorial is one of the most visited sites in Washington, D.C.

A magazine from 1865 shows lawmakers celebrating the passage of the 13th Amendment.

Congress to pass the 13th Amendment. It said, in part, "neither slavery nor involuntary servitude . . . shall exist within the United States." By December 1865, three-fourths of the states had approved the amendment. Sadly, Lincoln was not alive to see it. A year later, Congress passed a law granting African Americans citizenship and equal legal protection.

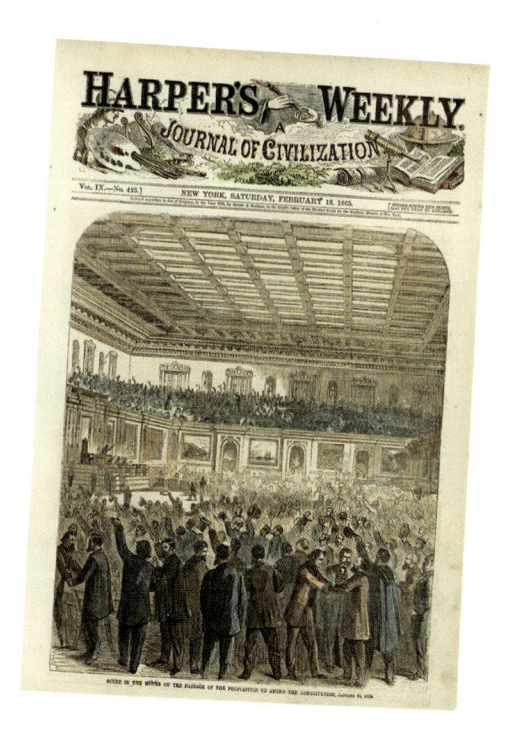

The 13th Amendment officially ended slavery. However, many of the problems and feelings raised by that shameful practice are still part of our lives today.

TIMELINE

American History

1809
James Madison takes office as the fourth U.S. president on March 4.

1842
On May 2, explorer John C. Fremont sets off on his first expedition of the Oregon Trail.

1854
On May 30, the Kansas-Nebraska Act replaces the Missouri Compromise for determining which states will allow slavery.

── 1809 ▶ 1842 ▶ 1854 ▶ 1860 ▶ ──

Abe Lincoln's Life

1809
Lincoln is born on February 12 in Hardin County, Kentucky.

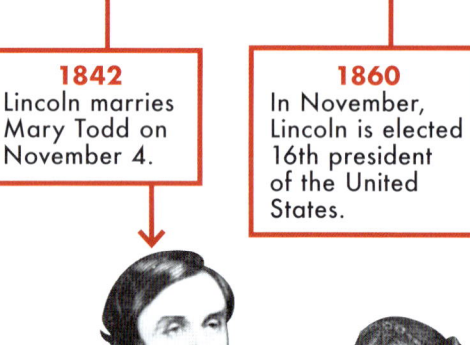

1842
Lincoln marries Mary Todd on November 4.

1860
In November, Lincoln is elected 16th president of the United States.

30

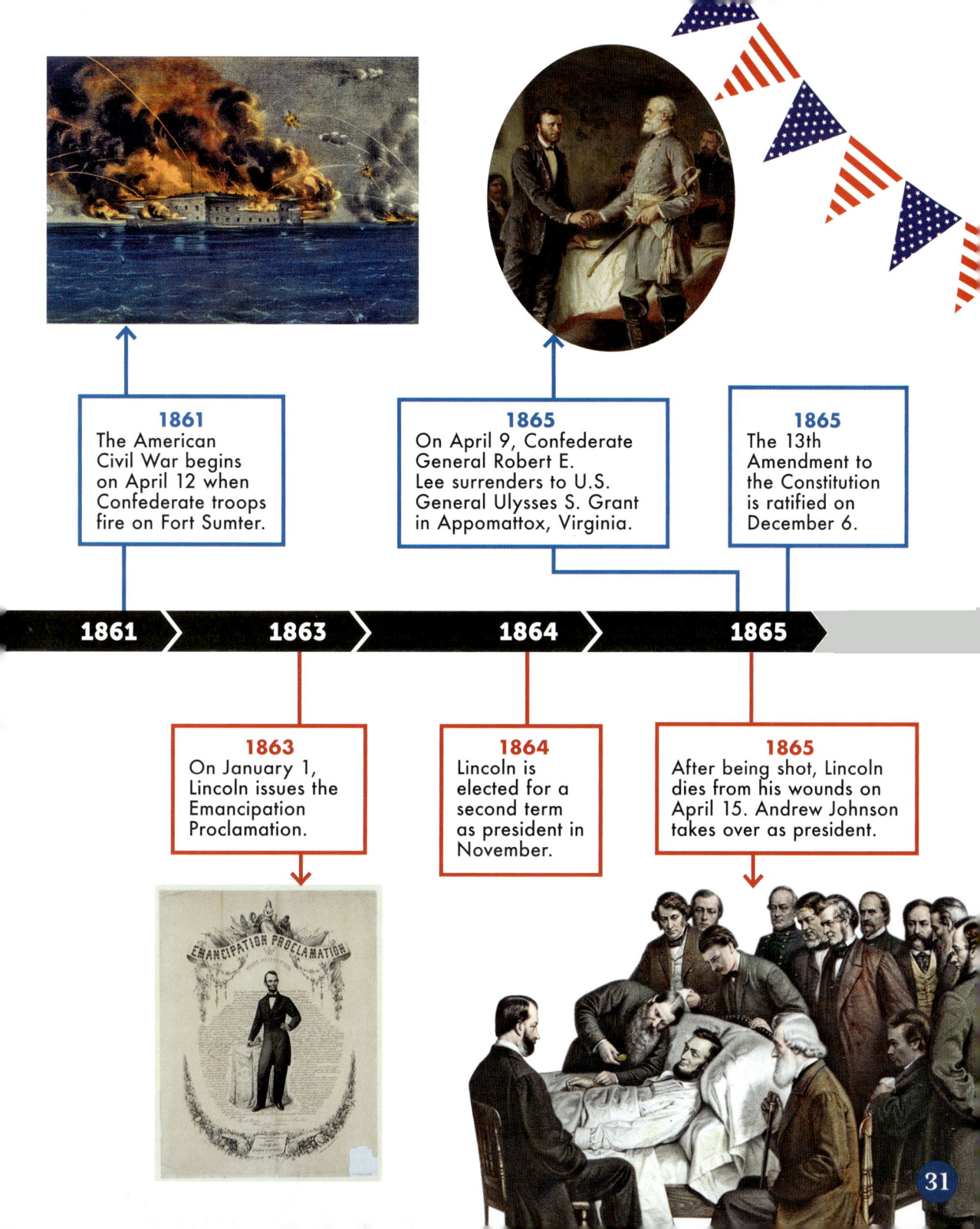

1861
The American Civil War begins on April 12 when Confederate troops fire on Fort Sumter.

1865
On April 9, Confederate General Robert E. Lee surrenders to U.S. General Ulysses S. Grant in Appomattox, Virginia.

1865
The 13th Amendment to the Constitution is ratified on December 6.

1861 › 1863 › 1864 › 1865

1863
On January 1, Lincoln issues the Emancipation Proclamation.

1864
Lincoln is elected for a second term as president in November.

1865
After being shot, Lincoln dies from his wounds on April 15. Andrew Johnson takes over as president.

31

GLOSSARY

abolished (uh-BAH-lished): put an end to officially

debate (di-BAYT): a discussion in which people express different opinions

emancipation (i-man-suh-PAY-shun): freedom from slavery

legislature (LEJ-is-lay-chur): a group that has the power to make or change laws

seceded (si-SEED-ed): formally withdrew

slavery (SLAY-vur-ee): a system in which people are owned by other people and thought of as property, without the right of fair treatment

term (TURM): a definite or limited period of time

INDEX

13th Amendment.......... 28–29
Booth, John Wilkes...27
childhood 7, 9
Civil War.................4, 17–27, 28
death 27
debates 9, 15
Douglas, Stephen......... 14, 15
early careers..9, 11, 12
Emancipation Proclamation......20, 21
family..........11, 20, 21
Gettysburg Address...................23
Kansas–Nebraska Act..........................15
Missouri Compromise 12, 15
presidency.........17–27
slavery 4, 12, 17, 21, 28–29

ABOUT THE AUTHOR

John Perritano is an award-wining journalist, author, and editor from Connecticut. He has written many books and articles on science, history, and current events. Perritano holds a master's degree in American history from Western Connecticut State University.